THE VISUAL
I CHING

D1443463

THE VISUAL
I CHING
A NEW APPROACH TO THE
ANCIENT CHINESE ORACLE

CARDS AND COMMENTARY BY
OLIVER PERROTTET

Salem House Publishers
Topsfield, Massachusetts

Text and cards copyright © Oliver Perrottet 1987
This edition copyright © Eddison/Sadd Editions 1987

All Rights Reserved. No part of this work may be reproduced or utilized
in any form, or by any means, electronic or mechanical including
photocopying, recording or by any information storage and retrieval
system, without the prior written agreement of the publisher.

First published in the United States by Salem House Publishers in 1987
462 Boston Street, Topsfield, MA 01983

Library of Congress Catalog Card Number:
86-62396

ISBN 0 88162 265 6

AN EDDISON · SADD EDITION
Edited, designed and produced by
Eddison/Sadd Editions Limited
2 Kendall Place, London W1H 3AH

Phototypeset by Bookworm Typesetting, Manchester, England
Origination by Columbia Offset, Singapore
Printing, binding and manufacture in Hong Kong by Mandarin Offset .

Contents

The ideas are expressed in pictures
the pictures are explained in words

Clinging to the words
we fail to understand the pictures
clinging to the pictures
we fail to understand the ideas

Having understood the pictures
we can forget the words
having understood the ideas
we can forget the pictures

Wang Pi (226-249 AD)

INTRODUCTION

*W*hen I first came across the I Ching, at the age of 22, I was not at all attracted by it. I knew a number of people who used to toss coins from time to time and then looked up the result in a book where, they told me, they would find the answers to their very personal questions. When I asked them who had written the book and how it worked, they did not know, nor did they care, they just knew how to consult the 'oracle'. I wondered how they could get meaningful answers from a source they used like a humble cookery book and I did not like the idea of it. If it really was a 'book of wisdom' surely one should have to do more than simply toss coins in order to merit a share in its knowledge?

I paid little attention to the subject, until one day, a relative gave me a newspaper cutting he had saved for me, because he knew I was interested in 'Chinese stuff'. It was a review of an I Ching translation that had just been published, and was illustrated with a whole page of strange looking signs, each composed of six horizontal lines. Some of the lines were broken, others not, but each sign seemed to be different from all the others. It seemed there was a symbolic language and possibly also a structure behind that obscure book.

I immediately bought a copy of the new edition and started studying. From the short introduction and from other sources, as well as by drawing my own conclusions, I started learning something of the history of I Ching, the Book of Changes.

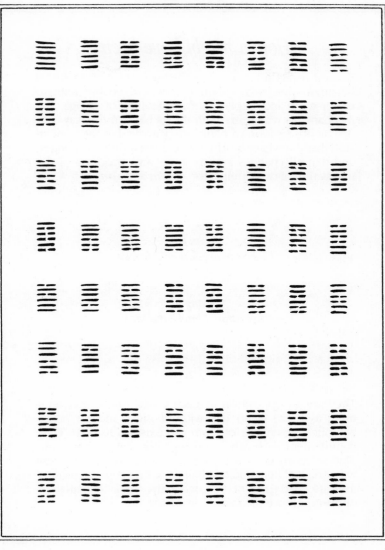

How it might have been

Several thousand years ago, the sages of ancient China began to design a system that would enable man to understand and explain the mutability of things, the mechanisms which make all things happen the way they do. By observation of nature they arrived at the conclusion that the whole world is one eternal flow of changes, and that all changes are, in some way, products of the interaction of two original forces: *Yin* and *Yang*.

Yin is
passive, weak, dark and female

Yang is
active, strong, bright and male.

Yin and Yang stand for all the contrasts in this world. They are in opposition to each other, but at the same time, as there is no day without night and no peace without war, neither of them can exist on its own. They complement each other and together make a new unit. This relationship was represented as a symbol: a circle with one half light and one half dark. The contrasting dots indicate that each of the two halves also contains its opposite. Hence the mutual attraction.

*I*n writing, the two contrasting forces were represented as lines, a broken line for Yin and an unbroken line for Yang.

From this, the laws of polarity were formulated: to every unit there is an opposite unit. These two complement each other and form together on a higher level, a new unit. The latter in turn finds its complement with which it forms, on a still higher level another new unit, and so forth. Vice versa, every unit can be divided into two complementary units, of which each can be subdivided into two again, and so on, infinitely.

The intricate system that results from such continuous division was exactly what the ancient sages were looking for, because in this way, complexity could be reduced to a simple and understandable polarity.

*T*he division of the two original forces produced four forces: Yang was divided into Yang/Yang and Yang/Yin, while Yin was divided into Yin/Yang and Yin/Yin. In writing, another line was simply added to the first one.

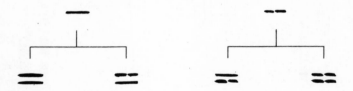

The four resulting signs were associated with the four directions of the heavens.

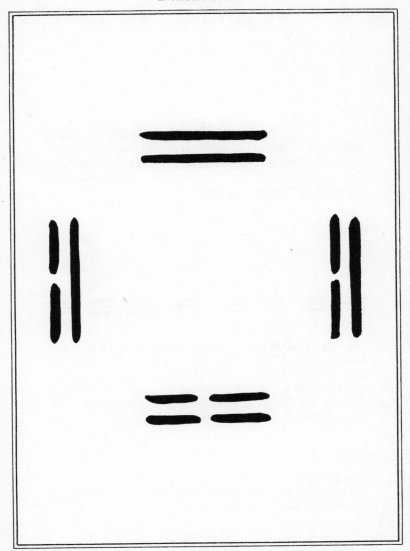

*I*n order to refine the system still further, the four forces were divided once more: From Yang/Yang came Yang/Yang/Yang and Yang/Yang/Yin, and so on. Thus a third line was added and eight signs called *trigrams* emerged.

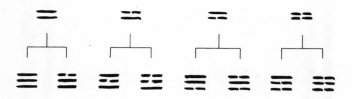

The sages named the eight signs after nature: Heaven and Earth, Fire and Water, Thunder and Wind, Mountain and Lake. Everything in the world could be fitted into their scheme, and for the time being, no further refinement was needed. Scholars began studying the meanings of the trigrams and their applications in life.

General note
All signs of I Ching are read from *bottom to top* and, if arranged in a circle, looked at from the centre.

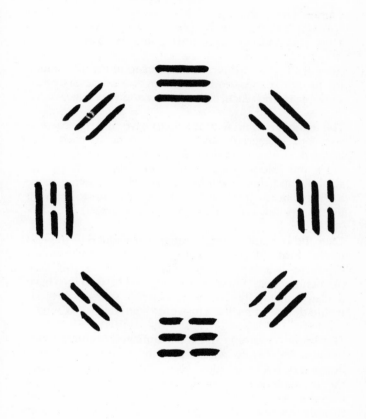

*B*ut as one force on its own cannot effect change, the scholars soon started to combine the trigrams by placing one above the other. Thus sixty-four combinations could be formed.

After having read this, I looked again at the illustration in the newspaper, and there they were: the sixty-four signs of six lines each, called *hexagrams* (see page 9).

The legendary king Wen is said to have first recorded all sixty-four hexagrams and given a name to each, thus laying the foundation stone for the Book of Changes. The sages and rulers of succeeding generations studied the symbols and their meanings thoroughly, drawing more interpretations from them. Rulers began to consult I Ching seeking counsel for their official duties.

Over the centuries, new findings were added to the text in the form of commentaries. The great philosopher Confucius was among the many authors of this supplementary text. When he was very old he is said to have declared that, if he had a further fifty years to live, he would devote himself exclusively to the study of I Ching.

The book containing these accumulated commentaries became ever more widely known. It survived a great burning of books (around 220 BC) and gradually became the instrument of popular soothsayers. Inevitably, this brought with it a new flood of commentaries and hypotheses. Soon, the original sixty-four hexagrams and the brief text of the ancient sages seemed doomed to be swamped amidst spurious fair-ground nonsense.

But in the third century AD Wang Pi, a young scholar who died at the age of twenty-three, vigorously opposed this development. In his writings he showed that the value of I Ching lay, not in its appeal as a fortune-telling device, but in the sixty-four original hexagrams and the ideas concealed within them – ideas which everyone has ultimately to work out for himself.

When I read this I felt great sympathy for the young scholar. Was that not the same way I had been feeling about I Ching?

In 1923 I Ching appeared in the West, translated by the German sinologist Richard Wilhelm. His excellent translation was highly acclaimed but hard to understand for the average reader. Subsequently, other versions appeared in other languages and distinguished thinkers of the twentieth century such as C.G. Jung and Hermann Hesse became deeply involved with I Ching.

But soon, a development similar to that in China 2,000 years ago, began. More and more commentaries and modern offshoots (the I Ching Calendar, the Medical Book I Ching, the Computer I Ching and so on) appeared in numerous Western languages, and the Book of Changes became known again all too quickly as a book of fortune telling.

'Why did this happen?' I asked myself. Why did people prefer just *one* side of the book, the unconscious, mystical one, and not care at all about its conscious, logical side – its basic structure formed by the sixty-four hexagrams?

There was a simple answer: the prospect of getting answers to all of one's questions from an old 'book of wisdom', just by tossing coins or performing a similar ritual, seems highly attractive, especially to many spiritually insecure inhabitants of the West. And performing such a ritual does not require great skill, nor much time, nor even faith.

But to get involved with the essence of I Ching, the system of the sixty-four hexagrams and the universal laws hidden within them which determine the course of our existence – that is a completely different matter. It means being conscious of all the hexagrams, their meanings and relationships, all at once. Something like playing chess in one's head.

At this point it occurred to me that if I had a card to represent each sign I would not have to do it all in my head. I would be able to interrelate the signs by moving the cards around. By playing with the cards physically on a table, I could *visualize* everything! Not only that, with a symbolic picture and a specific colour on each card, I would even get rid of those confusing broken and unbroken lines . . .

So the idea of the I Ching picture cards was born.

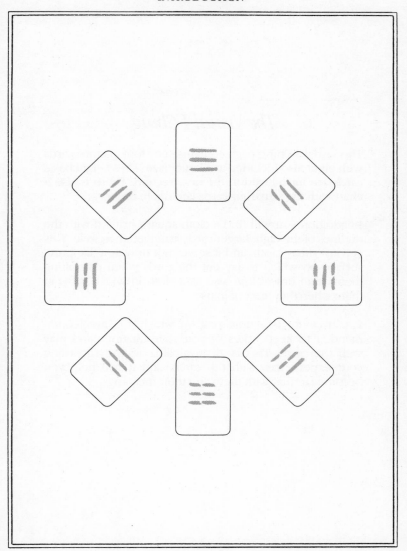

The Visual I Ching

The Visual I Ching pack contains sixty-four picture cards with eight also included at a larger size. These eight basic cards are introduced in the next section. There is also a chart with the sixty-four cards laid out in order.

In addition you will find a cloth square printed with the outlines of the eight larger cards arranged in a circle. This is your 'ritual' cloth, and it serves not only as a flat 'pure' surface on which to lay out the cards when consulting them as an oracle, but also as a cloth in which to wrap them when they are not in use.

Finally, there is a note pad on which you are recommended to keep notes of your consultations and play with the cards. This is an invaluable way of recording your experiences with the cards, and it will help you become familiar with them and their meanings.

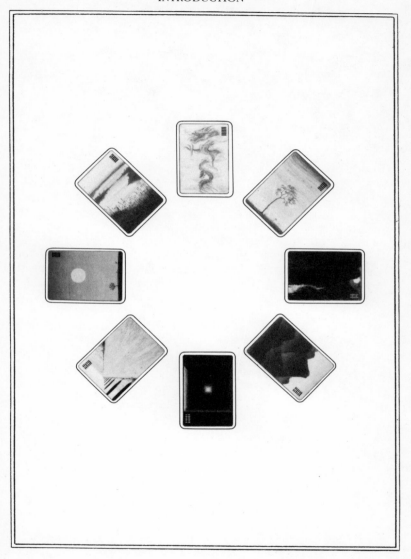

THE EIGHT
BASIC CARDS

*T*he traditional trigrams have turned into cards, but their meanings and their order remains the same. Laid out in a circle, we still observe four pairs of opposites, one pair on each axis:

On the vertical axis, HEAVEN and EARTH are shown as *Dragon* and *Square*, in white and black.

On the horizontal axis, FIRE and WATER are represented by *Sun* and *Moon*, in orange and blue.

On one diagonal axis, WIND and THUNDER appear as *Tree* and *Road*, in green and yellow while, MOUNTAIN and LAKE symbolize themselves in violet and red.

These eight basic forces and the nature of their interactions are the principal subject of I Ching. Getting to know each one of them will be the first step for anyone who wishes to enter the world of the Book of Changes.

Note that one basic card can have many different names or meanings, according to the context it is placed in. For instance, the name HEAVEN refers to the context 'nature', but the same card will be called 'Father' if looked at in the context 'Family', 'Strength' as an 'Expression', or 'Horse' on an 'Animal' level, and so on. The following pages offer an overall view of corresponding meanings for each basic card. By exploring patiently all the different aspects, you will gradually develop a personal relationship with each card and thus be able to *feel* its essence, which cannot be expressed in words.

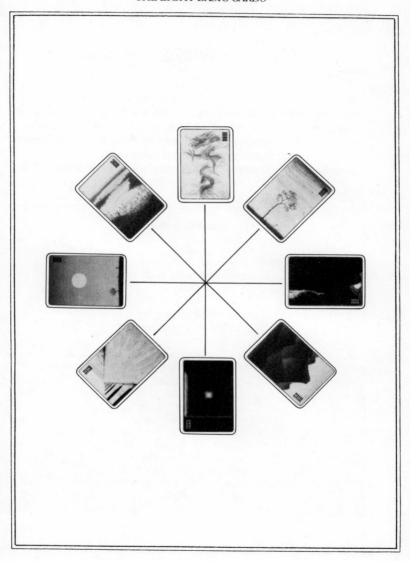

Heaven — Earth: the vertical axis

*T*he dragon is to the Chinese a
*legendary creature of heavenly origin, which moves through the air at great
speed. It has power over the course of water and is therefore an object of
reverence. From ancient times, it has been a symbol of wisdom and dignity.
It embodies the creative Yang-principle.
The square represents the measurable surface, earth, matter. It embodies the
receptive Yin-principle.*

Heaven is also:

father
active, creative, firm, straight and round, limitless, empty
reason, strength, durability
head
horse
cold and ice
ruler, outer garment
fruit from a tree

Earth is also:

mother
passive, receiving, yielding, patient
fertility, fulfilment, dedication, modesty
belly (which gathers and distributes everything anew)
ox, cow, and calf, mare
big cart or large spread-out cloth
(which carry all things without distinction)
tree trunk

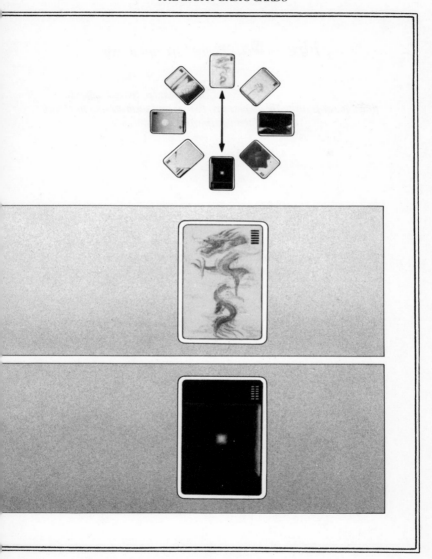

Fire — Water: the horizontal axis

*F*ire *appears in heaven, water is drawn towards earth. The Chinese say: heaven and earth act and meet each other through fire and water.*

Fire is also:

middle daughter
bright, clear, luminous, clinging, hollow, dry
light, beauty, elegance, intelligence, logic, knowledge and speech
eye
pheasant
sun, lightning
fat-bellied people, hollow objects (such as shells and armour)
dry trees

Water is also:

middle son
dark, abysmal, dangerous, penetrating, damp or wet, crooked
difficulty, defilement, erosion, instinct, desire, fearlessness
ear
wild boar
river, rain, moon
bend, thief
marrowy wood

Thunder – Wind: the first diagonal axis

*T*his is the axis of movement. The road means movement, noise, violent jolting. All this is reminiscent of thunder, which in the Chinese imagination erupts from the depths in early spring, awakening the seeds and starting a new cycle of life. The tree, too, moves, but only in itself. Being firmly rooted in the earth, it bends gently in the wind.

Thunder is also:

eldest son
violent, determined, shaking, exciting,
extending in all directions
energy, execution, awakening, burst of passion, will, spontaneity
foot (serves for motion)
dragon (which embodies the male principle)
earthquake, volcano
reed (which shoots up quickly)

Wind is also:

eldest daughter
gentle, adaptable, flexible but tough
progress, perseverance, dissolution, justice, charity
thighs (serving motion as impulse)
cock or tiger
wood, scent
people bent on profit
high and tall trees

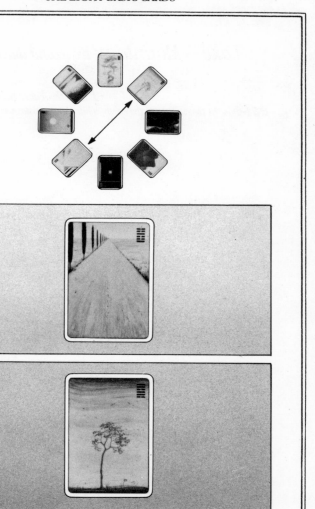

Lake – Mountain: the second diagonal axis

This is the axis of tranquility. The lake is a hollow in the surface of the earth, while the mountain is an elevation of it.

Lake is also:

youngest daughter
joyous, inviting, tender but hard at the core
attraction, pleasure, satisfaction, sensuality
mouth, lips (which smile and speak)
sheep
mist, harvest
concubine, sorceress
hard and salty earth (at the bottom of a dried lake)

Mountain is also:

youngest son
quiet, calm, earnest
stillness, withdrawal, turning away, meditation, concentration, void
fingers and hand (which hold things tightly)
dog
door, opening, small path, small stones
watchman
strong and gnarled tree

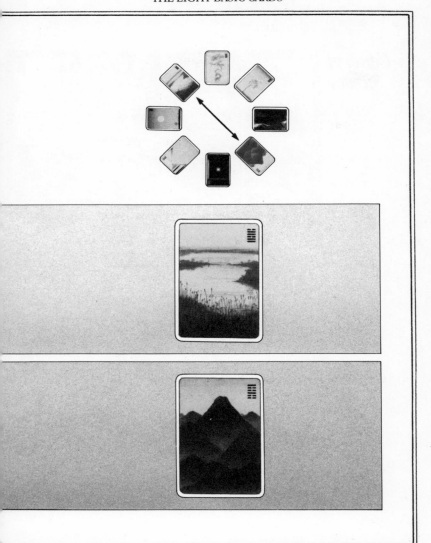

General Survey				
Name	HEAVEN	LAKE	FIRE	THUNDER
Colour	white	red	orange	yellow
Trigram	≡	≛	☲	☳
Family	father	youngest daughter	middle daughter	eldest son
Oracle line	—	--	--	—
Properties	active creative firm	joyous inviting tender	bright clear clinging	violent trembling extending
Expression	reason strength durability	sensuality pleasure satisfaction	beauty elegance intelligence	energy awakening execution
Body	head	mouth	eye	foot
Animal	horse	sheep	pheasant	dragon
Others	ice	mist	lightening sun	volcano

WIND	WATER	MOUNTAIN	EARTH
green	blue	violet	black
eldest daughter	middle son	youngest son	mother
gentle flexible tough	abysmal penetrating fearless	quiet calm earnest	passive receiving patient
progress dissolution justice	difficulty defilement instinct	stillness withdrawal meditation	fulfilment dedication fertility
thigh	ear	hand	belly
cock	boar	dog	ox
wood	rain moon	door	big cart

*F*or a start, arrange the eight basic cards (the large cards) in a row as shown below. In this sequence, their colour scheme becomes apparent: the six middle cards form a rainbow, stretching between Heaven and Earth, the two cards at the beginning and the end of the row.

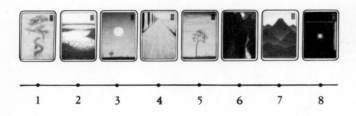

1	2	3	4	5	6	7	8

Now change the linear arrangement into a circular one as shown opposite. Start at the top with HEAVEN and move downwards along the left hand side. Then following the dividing line up through the centre of the circle and move downwards along the right hand side, until you reach the bottom, EARTH. This circular arrangement is probably as old as the eight trigrams, and it throws some light on the origin of the Yin/Yang symbol.

The basic cards have now been introduced to you. You can learn to relate to them just as if they were people and develop a personal relationship with each one of them. Some will remain mere acquaintances, others may become close friends.

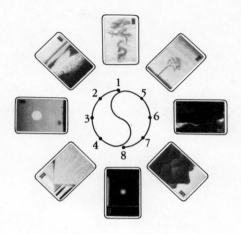

General note
Whenever working with the cards, use the large cards when only basic forces are involved, and the small ones where there are combinations of forces (see end of next chapter).

THE ORACLE

Consultation of the oracle is not a party game. It is an act to be taken seriously and should only be attempted when the necessary preliminary knowledge has been acquired, that is, the meanings and relationships of the eight basic forces.

Perform the consultation as a ritual. This will help to create the atmosphere of tranquility and concentration that is needed.

The issue

You may have a concrete question in mind to which you seek an answer; giving a direct answer to a direct question does not exhaust the oracle's capacity. Let it *comment on an issue* instead. Remember that it is you yourself who ultimately provides the answer by your interpretation of the oracle.

Once the issue or question is formulated you may put it down in writing. In any case, keep your mind concentrated on the subject while creating the answer. If no specific issue is presented to it, the oracle will simply comment on your present situation. Likewise, if the formulated question or issue is a superficial one, I Ching may comment on a subject the questioner is *really* worrying about at the time of the consultation.

Creating the answer

Place the ritual cloth in front of you, and put the eight basic cards on it, face down. Mix them for a while with uniform hand movements, gradually bringing them into the circular formation indicated. When the circle is formed, select a card at random and turn it over. Note the *name* of the card (LAKE, WIND, etc.) and then put it back with the others, face down as before. This procedure (mixing, forming a circle, making notes of the selected card) is then repeated another five times, ie six times in all. Line by line, you are creating one of the sixty-four hexagrams.

Example:

6. WIND
5. HEAVEN
4. MOUNTAIN
3. EARTH
2. MOUNTAIN
1. LAKE

Note that the cards are listed from *bottom to top*, number 6 the last to be drawn.

Building the hexagram

A line-hexagram can now be formed, in accordance with the following pattern: the 'male' cards are represented by a Yang-line, the 'female' cards by a Yin-line.

HEAVEN	(father) ━━━━━ *	EARTH	(mother) ━━ ━━ *
THUNDER WATER MOUNTAIN }	(sons) ━━━━━	WIND FIRE LAKE }	(daughters) ━━ ━━

From the example shown you will thus obtain the hexagram (a).

Changing lines:

When either or both of the extremes, ie HEAVEN and/or EARTH, are involved, the respective lines which represent them can also become their opposite. We thus obtain a second hexagram (b).

		(a)	(b)
6.	WIND	━━ ━━	━━ ━━
5.	HEAVEN	━━━━━ * →	━━ ━━
4.	MOUNTAIN	━━━━━	━━━━━
3.	EARTH	━━ ━━ * →	━━━━━
2.	MOUNTAIN	━━━━━	━━━━━
1.	LAKE	━━ ━━	━━ ━━

Dividing the hexagram

As shown in the introduction, every hexagram is formed by two trigrams, and each trigram represents one of the eight basic forces. For convenience, the scheme is repeated here:

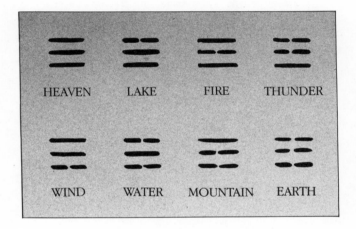

HEAVEN   LAKE   FIRE   THUNDER

WIND   WATER   MOUNTAIN   EARTH

Accordingly, our hexagram (a) depicts the combination WATER/LAKE (as always, reading from bottom to top), and the hexagram (b) the combination WIND/THUNDER.

This is where the 'combination' cards (the small cards) come in. With the aid of the chart supplied separately, locate the combination card that corresponds to the hexagram(s) you have formed and select this card from the pack.

WATER/LAKE

WIND/THUNDER

Interpretation

Place the resulting combination card in front of you and contemplate it. Let your gaze wander slowly from the bottom upwards and try to 'feel' the interplay of the two forces that are involved.

In the case of our example, WATER/LAKE, you might first imagine yourself to be advancing through a narrow and dangerous valley where you have to use all your skill and strength, and then to arrive in an open space where you can relax and rest.

If you have obtained a second hexagram by drawing HEAVEN or EARTH, this too is to be interpreted in the same way. Although the first card represents the actual answer, the second card provides a further illustration and puts the oracle's response into a larger context.

Now refer to the summary at the end of the book. There, for each combination card you will find:

● a short description of the contents of the card which illustrates the interaction of the two forces involved

● the resulting *meaning* of the card

● suggestions as to a correct attitude in this particular situation.

Only the most important points are noted in the summary. You will want to move forward from this base, throwing your own thoughts into the exercise. In order to do so, it will be useful to go through the games and exercises that follow on page 51, as this will deepen your understanding of the symbols as well as extending your base for interpretation.

Important: in the text of any complete I Ching translation you will find special commentaries on the 'changing lines' of each hexagram.

Combination cards

As the oracle demonstrates, the combination cards show the interplay of two basic forces. Each force encounters each of the others, giving rise to sixty-four possible combinations (8 x 8). Both forces, the one that is retiring and the one that has newly arrived, are part of the result, in the same sense as two relay runners share the responsibility for 'handing over the baton'.

In eight of these sixty-four encounters, however, one force meets itself, and the familiar basic cards result. They are in fact also combination cards, but enjoy a special status, representing a force which repeats itself and therefore doubles its effect.

General note
All cards are read from bottom to top. That is why the sequence is important. An inversion produces a totally different picture (see demonstration opposite).

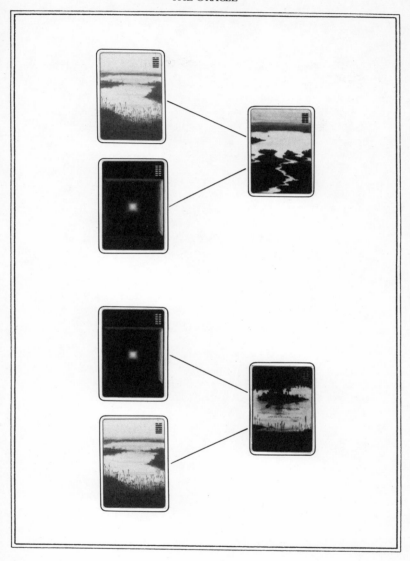

GAMES
AND EXERCISES

For everybody

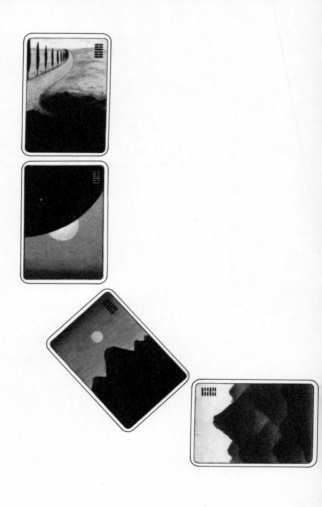

The following games and exercises will help you to get acquainted with all sixty-four cards. The first two games are easy and entertaining and therefore especially suitable for children.

Domino

The sixty-four cards are well shuffled and stacked face down on the table. Each player takes a card in turn, up to a certain number, say about eight. The cards are held in the hand hidden from fellow players. A player who holds a basic card (eg MOUNTAIN/MOUNTAIN) starts the game by

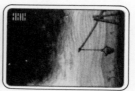

placing the card face up in the middle of the table. The next player lays a matching card (eg MOUNTAIN/FIRE or THUNDER/MOUNTAIN) above or below the first card. It is then the next player's turn, and so on. The cards must always point in the same direction, and should not stand on their heads. If a player has no matching card in his hand he takes another from the stack, and if he still cannot play, misses a turn. The game is finished when a player has got rid of all his cards or when none of the players can add a matching card.

Domino can be varied in many different ways by additional rules such as: if a player is unable to continue playing, he must go on taking from the stack until he draws a suitable card. Or, a number of matching cards can be played consecutively by the same player during his turn.

Interpretation:

At the end of the game, you may observe the complete card sequence and follow its evolution (with the aid of the sixty-four-card-summary at the end of the book). Of course, this can also be done during the game, while the chain of changes is still forming.

Memory

Lay out a quadrangle of eight times eight cards, face down. The first player turns up a card. He now has to find, by turning up another card, the one which makes its opposite (eg the card WATER/MOUNTAIN pairs with MOUNTAIN/WATER, WIND/WIND belongs to THUNDER/THUNDER, and so on). If he succeeds, he may keep both cards and pick up two more. If he does not, ie if the cards do not go together, they are placed face down again *in the same place as before*, and it is the next player's turn.

An easier version can be played in which both upturned cards need only agree in one picture half (eg LAKE/FIRE fits every other card which shows LAKE at the bottom). A more difficult game develops when the card to be found must be the complement of the first one, according to the four pairs of basic forces (eg HEAVEN/WIND then requires EARTH/THUNDER; see chart for reference).

Interpretation:

Names and meanings of the cards that are drawn can be brought into the game, and so a player's success or failure in finding the 'matching card' can be interpreted.

The Square

This can be played in a way similar to 'Domino', but the aim is to create a square formation rather than a chain of cards. The cards are laid out according to the following rules:

a) the cards must touch each other at least on one side
b) cards in horizontal rows must correspond in their lower halves
c) cards in vertical rows must correspond in their upper halves (see illustration)

The game is finished when a square formation of eight by eight cards has been completed. The aim for each player is, however, to be rid of all his cards and at the same time to hinder fellow players from off-loading theirs.

A meditative version for one player only:

Lay the cards out face down in an eight by eight square. Turn over a card at random and by referring to the chart determine its proper place within the formation. Put it there, take up the card which it replaces and put this one in its rightful place. Continue until all cards are in their correct positions.

Interpretation:

As you are playing, consider the meaning and interplay of the forces involved on each card. Try to see the correspondence between cards in the same row, ie with corresponding upper or lower halves.

The Square Arrangement

The square is the symbol of the earth. The Square Arrangement of the sixty-four hexagrams is as old as the hexagrams themselves. The formation as a whole reflects the network of their interrelations. Its sequence begins at the lower right corner with HEAVEN/HEAVEN and ends at the upper left corner with EARTH/EARTH. Between them, the other six basic cards form the diagonal a–b. The other diagonal from top right to bottom left (c–d) shows all combinations of the basic forces with their opposites.

Lay the cards out in Square Arrangement as shown opposite and on the chart. Practice several times, until you are able to do this without consulting the chart at all. In this way, you will get a feel for the position of each card which will be useful for further experiments.

When the formation is complete, contemplate it for a while. Then mix up the cards with a few quick hand movements, thus experiencing how a laboriously constructed order can be demolished in a moment.

At the end of each exercise, however, the cards should be collected and *put away in an order*. This can be either the order of the Square Arrangement, or in a personal order you devise for yourself.

When contemplating the Square Arrangement, you might also compare it with the first illustration in this book: the sixty-four hexagrams on page 9. Now, every hexagram has found its card.

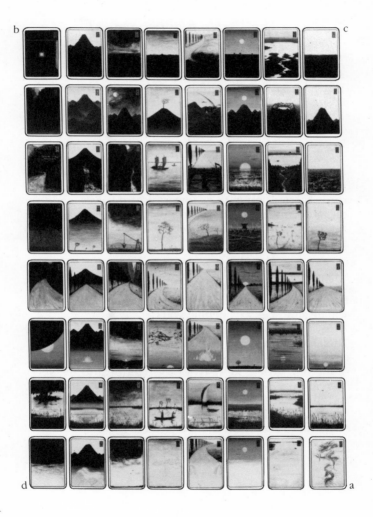

The Circle Arrangement

The circle is the symbol of the heavens. The Circle Arrangement of the sixty-four cards allows you to gain insight into the powerful system at the root of the cosmos. But we cannot survey the whole or comprehend it, for the circle represents the infinite.

In order to lay out the cards in the Circle Arrangement, you will need more space than an average table can offer, so sit down on the floor. As shown overleaf, make eight groups of eight cards each. Note that in each group all cards correspond in their lower picture halves, and that the groups are numbered from 1 to 8. Keeping to this sequence lay the cards in a circle around you (see next page).

Start with the first card of the first group, ie HEAVEN/HEAVEN, directly in front of you (a) and proceed anticlockwise to the last card of the fourth group, ie THUNDER/EARTH, which will lie almost exactly behind you (b).

Then follow an imaginary line through the centre of the circle, where you are sitting, and begin with the first card of the fifth group, ie WIND/HEAVEN, right next to the very first card (c). Now lay out the remaining cards clockwise and thus close the circle. The last card of all, ie EARTH/EARTH will lie directly behind you (d). Straighten the cards out so that a neat circle is formed.

Seated in the centre of a power field which was known to the Chinese of ancient times, you now experience I Ching in its entirety. You are at the intersection of the connecting lines between all opposites.

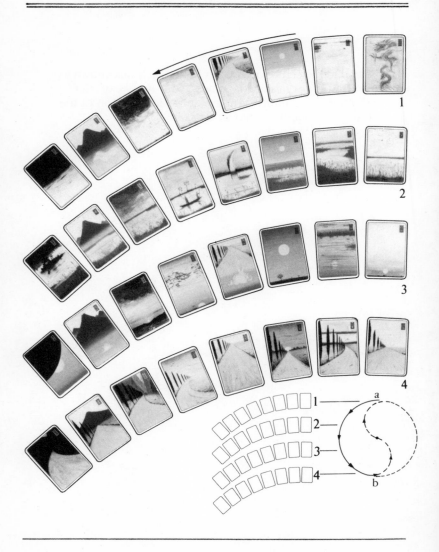

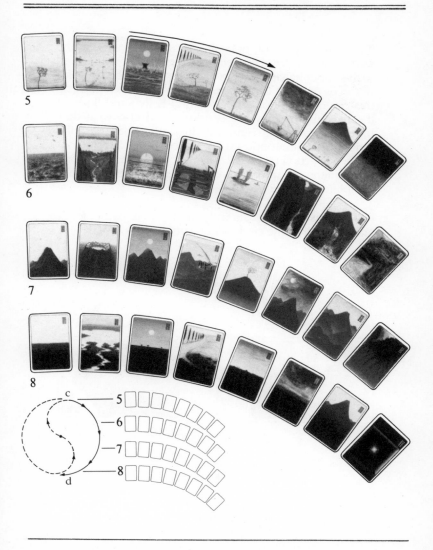

Take out a pair of opposite cards (eg FIRE/LAKE and WATER/MOUNTAIN) and contemplate them: the lower as well as the upper halves are opposites. Try to feel the interplay of forces on each card, to remember their meanings (in this case: 'Revolution' and 'Youthful Folly') and find out the reason why they are *opposites*, and also what they have *in common*. Here for instance: both describe actions that are opposed to established patterns, but while one action is carried out consciously, the other one is spontaneous and instinctive. Results are therefore completely different.

Repeat this exercise several times. Then pause for a moment and let the circle act on you.

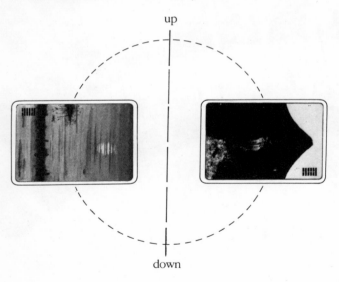

up

down

INSIDE AND OUTSIDE YOURSELF

The exercises of this chapter will show you how to get to know yourself, your partner, and your situation in general, by using the cards. It is also more essential here to 'feel' the meaning of each card, rather than just to understand it intellectually. Pay special attention to the paragraph 'family', for it will help you to achieve a specific relationship with each card.

Yourself

Form a sequence of the eight basic cards. First select the one you like best, then the second, and so on to the one you like least. If you find it difficult to establish a clear sequence, divide the cards in groups, a 'positive' and a 'negative' and perhaps an intermediate one.

In contemplating the eight cards, you will like some more than others, but it is easy to see that, in order to use them or play with them, you have to accept *all of them* as a whole. Not quite the same occurs with the different aspects of your own ego. You are open about the qualities you like, but might be inclined to conceal the ones you consider 'bad', even from yourself.

By doing so you inhibit your personality from full expression. Each one of us has experienced the conflicts which arise from giving the world around us an incomplete image of ourselves: difficulties in communication with others, the feeling of being misunderstood, and so on. By contemplating the sequence you have formed of the eight cards, you will be able to determine which parts of your own ego you prefer and which ones you tend to suppress.

Pay special attention to the latter ones. There is nothing wrong with not liking some aspects of your own self, but it is important to accept that they are there. Only then will it become possible to achieve a balanced personality.

Your preference for a certain card may vary from one occasion to another. From this you will pick up important clues as to your current state of mind and the changes that have occurred. However, you will always instinctively have a special relationship with one of the eight cards. Let us call it your *personal card*. Together with your *function card* (see paragraph 'Family') it is the card that represents yourself whenever you are communicating with I Ching.

Partnership

From among the eight basic cards, each partner selects his or her personal card. They place both cards between them, contemplate them and give reasons for their choice. Are there any aspects the two cards have in common? Are they opposites of some kind?

Then, they bring in the respective combination cards which can be formed from the two basic cards. The relationship between both partners can now be visualized from either side (see illustration: seen from FIRE's point of view, the relationship is symbolized by 'Beauty', from MOUNTAIN's point of view it is associated with 'The Stranger'). For further interpretation, consult the summary at the end of the book. Then discuss the two viewpoints and the nature of their interaction.

Alternatively, the exercise can be performed with the function cards (see the following exercise, 'Family') of each partner, instead of their personal cards.

Family

The eight basic cards constitute a family. HEAVEN and EARTH are father and mother. WIND, FIRE and LAKE, the three daughters, are turned towards the father, towards HEAVEN. THUNDER, WATER and MOUNTAIN, the three sons, are drawn to the mother, to EARTH.

Arrange the eight cards in a circle and contemplate them. Consider that, within a family, every member has a quite distinct function. Next to father and mother are WIND and THUNDER. They are the firstborn, the first of the children to take responsibility and, if necessary, to substitute the parents. THUNDER, the eldest son, is second to the father, and WIND, the eldest daughter, to the mother.

On the other side of each parent are MOUNTAIN and LAKE, the youngest children. They seek love and protection. MOUNTAIN, the youngest son, leans on the mother, and LAKE, the youngest daughter, on the father. FIRE and WATER, middle daughter and middle son, are in an intermediate position. They hold the balance within the family.

As the function a person performs within the family determines his or her development to a great extent, the family functions of the eight cards are a key to understanding yourself and your relationships with others. They also provide an important additional point of view for further studies of I Ching.

Contemplate the circle of eight cards and think of your own family in terms of the eight functions. Proceed by grouping the cards according to the status of each family

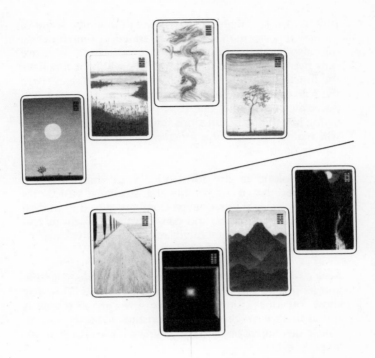

member.* Let the cards touch where there are close relationships and put them more apart where relationships grow more distant (see illustration on page 75).

* Of course, this exercise becomes even more revealing if other family members participate in it.

If there are less than eight persons in a family, some of them will perform more than one function. One function may also be shared by two or more persons: if there are only two sons, or two daughters, they will probably have the function of the eldest and youngest child, and share the role of the middle one between them. However, it is advisable to use only one card per person to start with, taking just the main functions into account. An only child will mainly perform the function of the middle son, or middle daughter.

When looking at the formation which has emerged, remember that it represents the structure which has shaped your own personality. Compare it to the original family circle formation and consider any distortions and missing elements. They might reveal to you the cause of conflicts among family members.

Now concentrate on the card which represents yourself, and its position in relation to the other cards. This may show you your position within *any* given group as well as reveal the nature of your relationships towards friends, colleagues, superiors and subordinates (see also exercise 'Exposure').

The card that symbolizes your function within the family will be called your *function card* (not necessarily identical with the already mentioned 'personal card'). Whenever you work with I Ching, the symbol this card contains will in some way represent yourself and therefore have a special significance for you. Its opposite in turn stands for the main issue you will have to deal with in life.

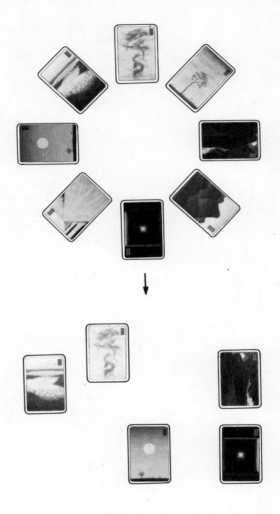

GAMES
AND EXERCISES

Not for everybody

The following exercises are for those who, after having thoroughly studied and understood the previous chapters of this book, wish to deepen their knowledge of I Ching still further.

Meditation

One method of learning to 'feel' the meaning of each card is through meditative contemplation. Meditating does not necessarily mean to be seated in the lotus position or to burn incense (although both make good sense). You simply place a card (later on you may want to use several cards at once) in front of you, contemplate it at leisure, and allow your thoughts to flow freely and without interruption. You can do this anytime and anywhere, you do not even need to have the card physically in front of you. For instance, you might try to do this while waiting at a bus stop.

The choice of a particular card for meditation can be made both consciously and unconsciously; you can:

Choose a card that attracts or repels you particularly; choose a card that seems to reflect best a given situation (eg the situation you are currently in); draw a card at random; or select a card by elimination

The most rewarding objects for meditation are the cards to which you do not find access at first, for they point to certain inner, as yet unknown, regions in the self.

Tracing the oracle

When consulting the oracle, and before you proceed to construct your hexagram, you might want, according to the taoist view of *way* and *aim* as being *identical*, to consider the cards which have produced the answer. Arrange them in a way that reflects the order of their appearance, and contemplate the formation. Recall the whole process, paying special attention to the cards that have appeared more than once. Also consider the forces which have not turned up at all.

The illustration shows on the left hand side the cards which led to our hexagram (see chapter 'The Oracle' page 41): LAKE/MOUNTAIN/EARTH/MOUNTAIN/HEAVEN/WIND.

The two elemental forces

Draw the Yin/Yang symbol on a piece of paper and lay the two cards, HEAVEN and EARTH, above and beneath the circle. Now think of different pairs of complementary concepts (they need not be traditional opposites), and relate them to the two cards, one to HEAVEN and the other to EARTH.

Examples:

question	answer
letter	number
teacher	student
bow	arrow
think	feel
laugh	cry
eat	drink
expand	contract
right	wrong
particular	general
silent	noisy
classic	romantic

and so on.

This sort of exercise makes us realise that the meaning of a card changes according to the context it is placed in. HEAVEN or EARTH are just names that embrace a multitude of different meanings. Names are labels we use to *identify* things, but they do not *define* them.

The four elements

Lay the four cards HEAVEN, EARTH, FIRE and WATER around the drawing of the Yin/Yang symbol. The twosome has become a foursome: the four elements.

Just as in the preceding exercise, think of other foursomes and relate them to the four cards. Examples: the cardinal points of the compass (with South on top, as represented by the ancient Chinese), the four seasons, temperaments, tastes, arithmetical operations, and so on.

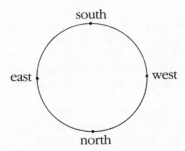

Alternatively, other foursomes can be created by inserting degrees between two opposites (as 'warm' and 'cool' between 'hot' and 'cold'), or by combining two opposed concepts. For instance, a certain idea may seem 'very attractive' (1), but from another point of view it may look 'highly dangerous' (2). Looked at from intermediate angles, the same idea will then appear as 'attractive, but also dangerous' (3), or 'dangerous, but also attractive' (4), thus completing the foursome. Just be aware, and similar examples will turn up by themselves in daily life.

The eight basic forces

While drawing the Yin/Yang symbol on a sheet of paper, as in the diagram on page 39, imagine the cards through which you pass, and feel how the action develops. Start at the top with HEAVEN. It gives the idea, the seed. LAKE stimulates to progress, in FIRE thought takes form, action is carried out through THUNDER. With WIND comes adaptation to what exists, the abyss at WATER calls for caution and perseverance, calm sets in at MOUNTAIN, and finally, in EARTH, the result of the whole process becomes apparent.

Perform this exercise several times, until you get the feeling of the thrusting Yang-phase that is followed by a restraining Yin-phase. After some time you may discover that you are making fairly good freehand drawings of the most difficult of all forms: the perfect circle.

Another drawing/meditating exercise is to execute the same drawing with two pencils, one in each hand. You may either start from top and bottom at the same time and move inwards, or vice versa, starting from the centre of the symbol. This time imagine how each force determines (and is determined by) its opposite. HEAVEN calls for EARTH, LAKE for MOUNTAIN, and so on.

Interaction

Choose two at random from the eight basic cards. Then look for the corresponding combination cards and contemplate them one after the other. Let your gaze wander slowly from the bottom upwards; feel how the initial force creates a certain situation, how the second force takes over this situation and moulds it with its own potential. On reaching the top ask yourself: what was the nature, what was the result of this interplay? In what way are the two forces characterized by their interaction? Repeat the exercise, exchanging *one* of the basic cards. Compare the resulting relationship with the first one. What differences can you find? Continue in this way.

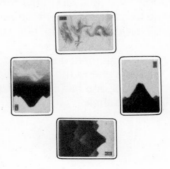

Note that two basic cards and their corresponding combination cards constitute a self-contained foursome. By positioning them as a quadrangle, a bright and a dark side appear, as in the Yin/Yang symbol. Use this holistic method whenever you are comparing two forces (see also exercises 'Partnership' and 'Four Elements').

Exposure

Choose one of the basic cards, eg your personal card or your function card. Then relate it successively to all other basic forces, just as in the foregoing example, using the corresponding combination cards. Eventually, you will end up with fourteen combination cards, seven of them showing the chosen basic force in their lower half, and seven in their upper half. Now arrange them in a double circle arrangement (see illustration but turn the page on its side), with the initial basic card in the centre. Note that in both circles all basic forces are in their correct order.

Contemplate this arrangement and use it for meditation. It allows you to comprehend the complete field of both action and reception of one basic force, exposing it, as it were, from all possible angles.

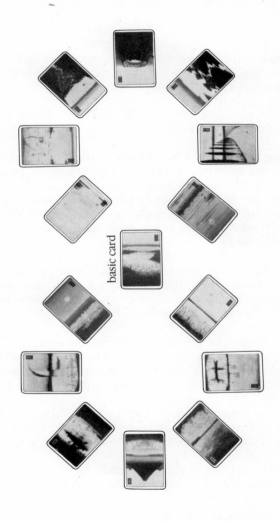

basic card

Chess

Chess and I Ching derive from common roots. This may be easily observed by looking at the Square Arrangement (chart) as if it were a chessboard.

White and black (HEAVEN and EARTH) define the two sides, the opponents in the game.

King and *Queen* on both sides have the positions of THUNDER and WIND, the eldest son and the eldest daughter. This explains why kings and queens stand directly opposite to each other (and not in symmetry to the centre of the board, as beginners often assume). The king is the leader of the army, at his side is the queen, his 'bodyguard'.

The *Bishops* are FIRE and WATER. Just like the two elements, they never meet each other, for each one moves exclusively either on white or on black squares. In the army, they are mediators and advisers.

The *Knights* or horses are LAKE and MOUNTAIN, the two youngest children of the family. Horses are valuable in battle but, as the youngest children, they do not act independently, and need guidance and careful handling.

The *Castles* are connected with HEAVEN and EARTH, father and mother. Like the parents in the family, they are the pillars which support the whole system.

HEAVEN and EARTH approach each other by LAKE and MOUNTAIN. Therefore, the white *Pawns* have LAKE, the black

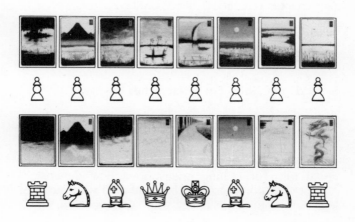

Pawns have MOUNTAIN as their common symbol. They are the vanguard of their armies, but, like the Knights who are also symbolized by LAKE and MOUNTAIN, they too are dependent. They act on orders and rely on support from the rear.

Not only the positions of chess figures are explained by the I Ching. Each square of the chessboard also acquires a special strategic value if related to its corresponding card in the Square Arrangement. You might confirm this by actually placing your chess figures on the chart (or on the cards laid-out in the Square Arrangement) and start playing. For instance, consider the initial moves of the Spanish opening, the most common of all openings:

First move: e2-e4. The field THUNDER is occupied by the advancing pawn. As you will remember, for the Chinese, Thunder gives the impulse which *sets things in motion* (see chapter THE EIGHT BASIC CARDS).

Black counters e7-e5, occupying the field DURATION, also meaning 'True Marriage': the attacking male principle is thus gently countered by the female principle.

Second move: Knight g1-f3, on to the field FIRE.

Black responds by: Knight b8-c6, on to the field WATER, and so on

For chess players, both beginners and advanced, the new visual form of I Ching opens up a new dimension. Abstract functions can now be combined with pictures, logic with intuition, strategy with contemplation, and a harmonious whole emerges. A chess player who is familiar with both ways of approaching the game might not only play chess with more awareness (and perhaps even more successfully), but also find his personal approach to the Book of Changes.

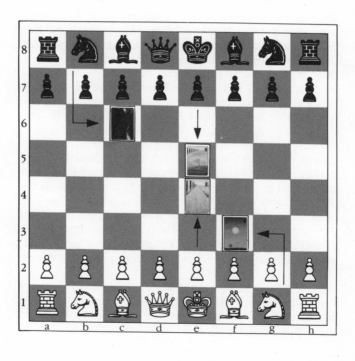

Extensions of games and exercises

The student who wishes to deepen his understanding of the Book of Changes will not allow himself to perform rigidly the same exercises all the time. He will change, extend and combine the examples given in this book, and find that I Ching provides limitless opportunities for unfolding his creativity.

The example opposite shows how to develop a given exercise: a second level is added to the exercise 'Partnership' (see chapter INSIDE AND OUTSIDE YOURSELF). Each partner selects not only his own personal card but also one for the other. The resulting four pairs of combination cards (the initial one, FIRE/MOUNTAIN and MOUNTAIN/FIRE, is not included in the illustration) show two ways of how the partners view themselves and two ways of how they are viewed by the other.

As well as chess, other board games such as draughts, Reversi (also called Othello) or Xiangqi (Chinese Chess) may be related to I Ching. Alternatively, a completely new game can be created. For instance, a game in which the players throw a dice and move their tokens along the chart according to their score. The meaning of each field they arrive at is discussed and will determine the player's further course of action. Role-playing games can also be imagined, with the eight basic functions providing the set of roles to choose from.

The editors will be delighted to receive suggestions on how to develop I Ching games and exercises still further, and to publish those ideas in a following edition.

THE SIXTY-FOUR COMBINATION CARDS

A summary

*T*he *following summary gives a short description of each combination card. Firstly, it illustrates the interaction of the two forces involved and the resulting meaning of the card. In a second paragraph, general advice is given on how to deal with the particular situation.*

Please note that only the most important points are summarized here. You will want to move forward from this base, throwing your own thoughts into your interpretations and conclusions so that you gradually establish a personal relationship with every card. The games and exercises suggested earlier have been devised to help you achieve this but as you do so, be patient with yourself for I Ching knows no haste.

HEAVEN/HEAVEN   *The Creative*

HEAVEN repeats itself. Continuous action of higher powers as well as of the superior being.

Follow the chosen path with calm, unfaltering steps. Act thus in harmony with the powerful, creative primeval principle, and success is assured.

HEAVEN/LAKE   *Breakthrough*

The power of HEAVEN has been shored up in the LAKE. It bursts out.

The good should be helped to succeed. Remain self-critical, inwardly strong and outwardly friendly. Do not apply force but take a firm and open stand.

HEAVEN/FIRE   *Possession of great things*

What HEAVEN gives to mankind becomes visible in the light of FIRE.

Encourage goodness and prevent evil. Such effort, undertaken with moderation and clarity, accords with the laws of Heaven and leads to great success.

HEAVEN/THUNDER   *Power of the Strong*

The strength of HEAVEN takes the form of MOVEMENT, and spreads itself out.

The way is free. Proceed with inner strength and a fine sense of justice. Thus there will be no deviation from your path.

HEAVEN/WIND   *Domination by Weakness*

The rising force of HEAVEN *is hindered by the gentleness of the* WIND.

Momentarily, weakness predominates over strength. This is achieved by gentleness and adaptability. The time has not yet come for energetic action so it is advisable to show restraint.

HEAVEN/WATER   *Waiting*

The rising force of HEAVEN *is facing* DANGER *in the form of rain clouds.*

Gather strength calmly and wait for fate to be fulfilled. Do not worry and take everything as it comes. If one does not deceive oneself, the path is clearly visible. Strengthen body and spirit. Perseverance brings success.

HEAVEN/MOUNTAIN   *Domination by Strength*

The power of HEAVEN *is bridled by the steadfastness of the* MOUNTAIN.

Focused strength enables you to do great things. Let these actions take effect outwardly, and be ready to make important decisions. Explore the past and learn from it.

HEAVEN/EARTH   *Peace*

The power of HEAVEN *strives upwards,* EARTH *downwards. Fertile union results.*

Contradictions unite in harmony. The strong help the weak. See to it that this situation bears fruit.

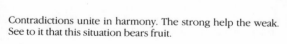

LAKE/HEAVEN   *Stepping*

The LAKE rises toward HEAVEN. The weak face the strong.

If the weak proceed courageously but respectfully and without evil intention, the strong will not be provoked. Recognise the inner nature of a person, and do not be impressed by external differences of rank.

LAKE/LAKE   *Serenity*

Two LAKES are linked together, and each one is fed by the other.

Associate with like-minded people to share experiences. Be inwardly strong and firm, outwardly mild and serene. Perseverance brings success.

LAKE/FIRE   *Opposition*

The coolness of the LAKE meets the heat of the SUN. Two sisters live in the same house but have opposing interests.

Men may have the same goals, but their ways often differ. Personal interests are emphasized, similarities with others recede. Only small projects can be realized.

LAKE/THUNDER   *The Marrying Girl*

The LAKE draws near to THUNDER. The young woman follows the older man into his house.

The situation is uncertain, an end is possible at any time. Adapt to the situation with tact and modesty. Do not venture on any new enterprise.

LAKE/WIND   *Confidence*

The WIND *wafts over the* LAKE. *The joyous meets the gentle.*

Approach everything and everyone cheerfully and gently. Recognise their inner nature and earn their trust. Take important decisions. Endurance brings success.

LAKE/WATER   *Measure*

The LAKE *is filled with* WATER. *The mouth speaks, the ear hears. Lake or ear do not have an infinite capacity.*

Undertake as much as you can master and no more, but also no less. Moderation brings success.

LAKE/MOUNTAIN   *Decrease*

The LAKE *dissolves. Mist rises and hides the* MOUNTAIN. *Thus both are weakened.*

Time of simplification, of poverty. Outer humility is no disgrace if there is inner substance. Quell lower feelings and muster your energy for higher things.

LAKE/EARTH   *Approach*

The LAKE *turns towards* EARTH, *the hollow strives towards its innermost centre. The youngest daughter approaches her origin, the mother.*

Take matters in hand. Perseverance brings success. Take heed quickly for circumstances may soon change.

FIRE/HEAVEN   *Community*

FIRE strives towards HEAVEN. The sun gives life and belongs equally to all beings.

Inside reigns clarity, outside strength. Differences between men may be overcome if exposed. Good partnership depends on common purpose. New ventures materialize, great deeds succeed. Perseverance brings success.

FIRE/LAKE   *Revolution*

FIRE and LAKE are in conflict, their interests oppose each other.

Choose the right moment for acting and the base for great innovations by careful observation of events. Perseverance brings success.

FIRE/FIRE   *Attachment*

Twice FIRE. The light is taken up by man and distributed further.

No man is independent, each clings to something, just as light does. Recognise and accept this dependance. It is important to serve in order not to become presumptuous.

FIRE/THUNDER   *Wealth*

FIRE meets with THUNDER and spreads out. Its warmth causes things to blossom.

Judge misdeeds shrewdly and punish severely. Only the genuinely strong enjoy times of prosperity. Decline follows later, but do not worry. Enjoy your wealth and share it with others.

FIRE/WIND   *Family*

FIRE engenders warmth, WIND spreads it. Thus many people share in it.

The family moulds a man's character, it teaches him how to deal with people. Perseverance and orderly conditions lead to success, disintegration of the family leads to decadence in society. Women, as the centre of families, bear a special responsibility.

FIRE/WATER   *After Completion*

The SUN sets, DARKNESS and RAIN arise, the day ends.

A deed has been achieved, the circle closed. Be satisfied but remain alert, otherwise all may be wrecked at the very last moment. Only small ventures have a chance of success.

FIRE/MOUNTAIN   *Beauty*

FIRE illuminates the MOUNTAIN. Within clarity and strength, without stillness and serene beauty.

Grace decorates and adorns but is often 'too beautiful to be true'. Do not make any important decisions, for they require a more realistic basis. Success is possible in small things.

FIRE/EARTH   *Eclipse*

The LIGHT is weakened or even obliterated by the EARTH.

Time of darkness and of need. Preserve inner clarity and strength, but show yourself externally flexible. Thus your real nature remains steadfast in difficult times.

THUNDER/HEAVEN   *Innocence*

THUNDER moves towards HEAVEN. The eldest son is outwardly a man, but to his father, he is still a child.

Act instinctively. Innocence is lost by any thought of personal gain, and misfortune follows at once.

THUNDER/LAKE   *Handing Over*

The violent movement of THUNDER changes into the pleasurable murmuring of the LAKE. It calms itself and gathers strength.

Time for repose and relief. The one who inherits a situation adapts to it. Start your work cheerfully, with conviction and good will. Perseverance brings success.

THUNDER/FIRE   *Biting Through*

THUNDER and LIGHTNING come together and split everything opposing them.

An impediment must be overcome, difficult matters sorted out. Identify errors and the ones to blame. Judge fairly and carry out decisions with firmness. Success is assured.

THUNDER/THUNDER   *Shock*

Repeated THUNDER. A shock first causes fear but then spreads out and brings 'good' vibrations.

Colossal movement. Do not be confused by initial fear but meet force with respect and composure. Turn inwards and bring order into your life.

THUNDER/WIND
Increase

The violence of THUNDER *is absorbed, reinforced and spread by* WIND.

Imitate the good and give up bad habits. Take important decisions and begin new ventures.

THUNDER/WATER
Initial Difficulty

The movement of THUNDER *leads to the* ABYSS.

Upon beginning a difficult task, one must prepare oneself well and arrange everything clearly in its proper place. Wait and see, call in helpers. Perseverance brings success.

THUNDER/MOUNTAIN
Mouth

The movement of THUNDER *is swallowed by the stillness of the* MOUNTAIN.

Practise moderation with words (sounds that leave your mouth) and with food and drink (energy which enters through it). Perseverance brings success.

THUNDER/EARTH
Turning Point

THUNDER *has retreated to its place of origin, deep into the* EARTH. *Now it moves upwards again.*

The old comes to rest, the new begins to move. New power, however, needs to be sheltered and given time in order to gain strength. New friends can help. (This is the last card of the first half.)

WIND/HEAVEN   *Concession*

The WIND *rises towards* HEAVEN. *The eldest daughter approaches the father, women approach men, the people approach their ruler.*

Two related but unequal forces. The weak approach the strong. A favourable opportunity to carry through a delicate measure. Caution is advisable, do not commit yourself.

WIND/LAKE   *Predominance*

The TREES *are underneath the* LAKE *which overflows its banks and inundates everything.*

The powerful predominates, and the situation becomes acute. Great changes are impending, be prepared and remain self-assured. Act gently, serenely, without hesitation.

WIND/FIRE   *Sacrifice*

WOOD *and* WIND *feed* FIRE. *Matter rises into the invisible. The sacrificial urn stands on fire.*

Give up something you cherish in order to dedicate it to a higher purpose. By submission you find your position in life and recognise your fate. Success will follow.

WIND/THUNDER   *Duration*

WIND *and* THUNDER, *submission and penetration, unite. Woman is inside and beneath, man is outside and above. A long-lasting union, the 'true marriage'.*

Duration means development, not stagnation. For development, space is needed. But it is important to have the goal in one's sights in order not to get lost.

WIND/WIND   *Gentle Penetration*

WIND meets WIND. It is gentle but penetrating and persistent.

Gentleness in word and deed lead to success. Obtain advice, explore the path thoroughly before following it.

WIND/WATER   *The Well*

The WOOD draws life-giving WATER from the earth and distributes it in all directions.

Get to the root of things. Work for the common good and help others. Let caution prevail, for the bucket with which you draw water is fragile.

WIND/MOUNTAIN   *Renewal*

The WIND encounters the MOUNTAIN and loses strength. Development stagnates and must be revitalized.

Discover the cause of problems and overcome them. Then there are good prospects for success. Wake up, gird yourself for a decisive step.

WIND/EARTH   *Striving Upwards*

WOOD penetrates the EARTH. A new plant has taken root.

The foundations of great things are built with painstaking effort. Seek advice but have self-confidence. Keep both path and goal in your sights. Success is assured.

WATER/HEAVEN   *Conflict*

WATER strives downwards, HEAVEN upwards. Father and son have different views.

Conflict arises when each party believes himself to be in the right exclusively. Do not take any important steps, nor try to finish your task now. Stop and seek advice.

WATER/LAKE   *Exhaustion*

The ABYSS opens in front of the LAKE. Distress before joy and deliverance.

Shortly before the goal a narrow gorge has to be overcome. Muster all your willpower. Big words do not help, no one believes them. Perseverance brings success.

WATER/FIRE   *Before Completion*

The SUN rises over the WATER. Evaporation will end the cycle.

A delicate situation demanding great caution. A mistake would be disastrous. Judge conditions with care.

WATER/THUNDER   *Relief*

Troublesome advance amid DANGER, followed by rapid MOVEMENT. The way is open.

A new beginning. Forgive your own mistakes and those of others. Settle quickly what has still to be done. After deliverance, do not run away, but find your way back to orderly conditions.

WATER/WIND   *Dissolution*

The WIND wafts over the WATER and ripples it. The dark, flowing force becomes bright and soft.

Selfishness evaporates and is sacrificed to a collective purpose. Human beings have mutual interests and therefore are united. A moment to take important decisions. Success through perseverance.

WATER/WATER   *Abyss*

WATER repeated. It flows on without interruption and does not shy away before the abyss. It changes its shape but not its character.

A dangerous situation. Behave like the water: be true to your inner self, do not stand still, do not be afraid. Act consistently.

WATER/MOUNTAIN   *Youthful Folly*

WATER bubbles up from the spring, seeming to depart from the MOUNTAIN. It does not yet suspect that at the end of its journey stillness awaits it again.

Much strength, but little experience. Recognise your situation and look for a teacher. Clear instruction is necessary. Avoid useless questioning. Perseverance brings success.

WATER/EARTH   *Army*

WATER is hidden in the EARTH. Inwardly danger hides, outwardly discipline rules.

Organisation and discipline are the most important elements. A strong leader can guarantee it, but only if he knows how to maintain good relations with his subordinates. Perseverance brings success.

MOUNTAIN/HEAVEN   *Retreat*

The MOUNTAIN *soars to lonely heights, above is only the emptiness of* HEAVEN.

Baseness gains ground, the superior one retreats with dignity. He feels no hatred for he is above ignoble emotions.

MOUNTAIN/LAKE   *Courtship*

The MOUNTAIN *bears the* LAKE. *The man courts the girl.*

Be receptive and assist other people, but remain steadfast and do not let yourself be seduced. Perseverance brings success.

MOUNTAIN/FIRE   *The Stranger*

The MOUNTAIN *stands motionless, above it the* SUN *wanders away.*

One is alone, having no permanent home and no circle of friends for support. Inner strength, outer modesty bring success.

MOUNTAIN/THUNDER   *Power of the Weak*

Powerful THUNDER *erupts from the silent* MOUNTAIN.

The small are able to do great things. Do not be over-ambitious, let caution prevail. Be content with achieving small successes.

MOUNTAIN/WIND   *Gradual development*

A TREE grows on the MOUNTAIN. Calm causes gradual development and organic growth.

Create orderly conditions. They are the necessary basis for all cooperation. But push forward gradually and constantly. A lack of perseverance may lead to stagnation.

MOUNTAIN/WATER   *Obstacle*

RAIN and DARKNESS are above the MOUNTAIN. Stand still in the face of danger.

The situation is difficult. Do not act but adapt to circumstances, keeping the goal in view. Be introspective, look for the fault in yourself. Seek advice.

MOUNTAIN/MOUNTAIN   *Keeping still*

MOUNTAIN above MOUNTAIN. Stillness pervades all.

Gather fresh strength through repose. Turn your thoughts inwards, away from material things. No error is possible if there is inner peace.

MOUNTAIN/EARTH   *Modesty*

The MOUNTAIN carries EARTH. What is high is brought down, what is low is raised.

Finish your work with modesty, do not expect fame. Weigh things up and balance them one with another. Success is assured.

EARTH/HEAVEN   *Stagnation*

The EARTH strives downwards, HEAVEN upwards. They divide and their interaction ceases.

Good recedes, evil increases. Retreat into your innermost self. By no means allow yourself to be enticed into participating in exterior life. Thus difficulties will be avoided.

EARTH/LAKE   *Gathering*

WATER collects on EARTH to form a LAKE.

Where people or things assemble much can happen. Start new ventures but be prepared for unforeseen developments. Make sacrifices, seek advice. Perseverance brings success.

EARTH/FIRE   *Progress*

The SUN wanders over the EARTH, bringing warmth and fertility.

Speedy, effortless progress. Strength will be richly rewarded if it is based on confidence and is not abused.

EARTH/THUNDER   *Enthusiasm*

THUNDER erupts out of the EARTH and awakens new life, as it happens in springtime.

Collect helpers around you and show your power. Do not fear an argument. Remember your faith and your origin.

EARTH/WIND   *Contemplation*

The WIND wafts over the EARTH, and gently strokes its surface.

By contemplating the world around you, recognise ways and means of influencing people and events. Make journeys, pay visits. Be a good example and mentor to others.

EARTH/WATER   *Holding Together*

WATER pours upon the EARTH and forms a connected system.

People can only hold together if each one sees himself as a member of a whole. Recognise your function in society, test your endurance and inner stature. For the insecure and hesitant it may get too late.

EARTH/MOUNTAIN   *Collapse*

A MOUNTAIN emerges where the EARTH folds itself. The ground is unsafe and may collapse at any time.

The situation is delicate. Only by making gifts to the lowly, can the great restore the balance and continue to exist. Do not undertake new ventures.

EARTH/EARTH   *The Receptive*

EARTH is vast. It carries good and evil with patience, there is room for everything.

Do not forge ahead but allow yourself to be led. Accept assistance at work, but advance alone in dealing with superiors. Perseverance combines strength and devotion, it brings success.

Acknowledgements

Oliver Perrottet would like to acknowledge his thanks to Doris Bendemann for providing a literal translation into English of the original German text, and to Yvonne Fürst for her assistance in editing the final English version.

Eddison Sadd Editions acknowledge the help of the following;

Creative Director Nick Eddison
Editorial Director Ian Jackson
Designer Amanda Barlow
Editors Charlotte Edwards and Christine Moffat
Production Bob Towell